A gift for:

From:

T0028178

OTHER HELEN EXLEY GIFTS
FOR FAMILY AND FRIENDS

365 For my Mother
Daily messages of thanks and love

365 For my Sister
A thoughtful message for every day

365 Happy Days!
A happy thought for every day

365 For my Grandma
Daily messages of love

365 Friendship
A thoughtful quote every day

365 For my Daughter
Daily messages of love

365 Mindful Days
A daily thought on being present in the now

365 Mothers & Daughters
Daily thoughts of care and love

365 For my Granddaughter
Daily messages of love

365 For my Dad, my Hero

You can order these lovely giftbooks on our website:
www.**helenexley**.com

For my special Son

Of all my friends
there is one I consider to be the best
and the dearest – my son.

BRIAN CLYDE

EDITED BY HELEN EXLEY
ILLUSTRATED BY JULIETTE CLARKE

Published in 2022 by Helen Exley® LONDON in Great Britain.
Selection and arrangement by Helen Exley © Helen Exley Creative Ltd 2022.
Words by Pam Brown, Charlotte Gray, Brian Clyde, Pamela Dugdale, Stuart & Linda
Macfarlane, Helen Thomson, Linda Gibson, Amanda Bell, Peter Gray, Odile Dormeuil,
Mathilde Forestier, Jane Swan are all © Helen Exley Creative Ltd 2022.
Illustrated by Juliette Clarke © Helen Exley Creative Ltd 2022.

ISBN: 978-1-78485-334-1   12 11 10 9 8 7 6 5 4 3 2 1

Helen Exley® LONDON
16 Chalk Hill, Watford, Hertfordshire, WD19 4BG, UK

You can follow us on and

For my special Son

My son lights the fire
of my deepest happiness
and fills me with such joy,
I feel my heart will burst.

GOLDIE HAWN

For my special Son

I would give you happiness if only I could.
But this is your life, your time,
and all I can give you is my advice –
strive for happiness and the world will be yours.

LINDA MACFARLANE

For my special Son

To watch your child grow
from a helpless baby
into a smart young man.
To feel that you have helped him
at each step of the way.
To know that you have shared
many precious moments.
These are life's real rewards...

LINDA MACFARLANE

For my special Son

I will work to make things
better for you.
But there are so many things
that I won't be able to solve.
And all I can do is to be here
for you. For life.

HELEN THOMSON

For my special Son

He makes fuzz come out of my bald patch!

CHARLES A. LINDBERGH

For my special Son

Thank you for making me feel life
is worth having whatever happens.

ODILE DORMEUIL

For my special Son

IF I HAVE A MONUMENT

IN THIS WORLD,

IT IS MY SON.

HE IS A JOY,

A SHEER DELIGHT.

MAYA ANGELOU

For my special Son

Sons walk away, ride away,
drive away, sail away. They always
have. But the steel-strong, web-fine
links that bind them to those
who love them and whom they love
in turn, cannot be broken. Ever.

PAM BROWN

For my special Son

You'll never know till you have a son of your own
how indecently proud parents are of their sons' achievements.
Of course I don't want you to be nothing but a clever swot
(there isn't the least danger of that!) but every time
I get news of your being top I throw a little chest
and go out and smile at the world.

RUDYARD KIPLING

For my special Son

When you are happy and when you are sad.
When you are celebrating and
when you are downhearted.
My love will be with you today and forever.

STUART MACFARLANE

For my special Son

I hope that your life leads through
a sunlit countryside. Adventures. Surprises.
And days of quiet content.
And friends for company. And the attainment
of your dreams – your secret hopes.

EDDIE MOLEFE

For my special Son

Thank you for being you.
For being there. For knowing how to do things
that baffle me. For rescuing me
time and time again.
What would I do without you?

HELEN THOMSON

For my special Son

I am here for you always –
proud of you, believing in you,
and hoping your dreams come true.

PAM BROWN

For my special Son

You light our lives.

I wish you discoveries and marvels.

I wish you success that has no sting.

I wish you joy and peace and

warm contentment.

And always, always, love.

EDDIE MOLEFE

For my special Son

Grow your own laughter. Catch your own dreams.
Fashion each day of your life
with excitement, joy and contentment.

AMANDA BELL

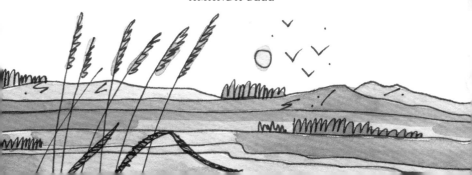

For my special Son

Joyful, kind, gentle,
fun-loving, loyal, sensitive,
patient, laughing, singing,
honourable, artistic,
home-loving, gorgeous –
our son.

CARON KEATING

For my special Son

We find delight in the beauty
and happiness of children
that makes the heart too big
for the body.

RALPH WALDO EMERSON

For my special Son

I wish you...
...the courage to choose
the difficult.
...the will to unravel the complex.
...new skills, new insights, new
adventures.
...the joy of always being astonished
by your own abilities.

KARABO FUNDE

For my special Son

Son, you entered my life and taught me how to smile again.
You showed me how to relax and have fun. Together, we made trips
to the moon, and conquered mountain ranges in the garden.
Life was never such an adventure till you came along.

STUART MACFARLANE

For my special Son

I saw pure love when my son looked at me,
and I knew that I had to make
a good life for the two of us…

SUZANNE SOMERS

For my special Son

Here are gifts for you.
Gulls scything the summer air.
Cats drowsing in sunlight.
Snow.
Laughter and song and friendship.
My gifts for you.
The gift of life.

ROSANNE AMBROSE-BROWN

For my special Son

A boy is a magical creature –
you can lock him out
of your workshop,
but you can't lock him
out of your heart.

ALAN BECK

For my special Son

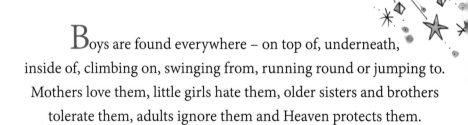

Boys are found everywhere – on top of, underneath, inside of, climbing on, swinging from, running round or jumping to. Mothers love them, little girls hate them, older sisters and brothers tolerate them, adults ignore them and Heaven protects them.

ALAN BECK

For my special Son

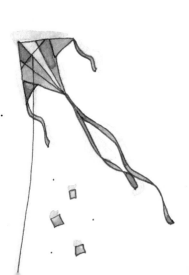

I am so proud of you.
Proud of your courage and your concern
for others, your resilience, your love of life.
Proud of all that you've achieved.
Your creativity. Your willingness to learn
– so much in one person!

CHARLOTTE GRAY

For my special Son

Words aren't enough to describe
the delight of fatherhood.
My children have given me the greatest happiness
in my life.

IMRAN KHAN

For my special Son

Walk proudly my son
Through life's joys,
songs and triumphs.
For my love will be there
in your heart.

LINDA MACFARLANE

For my special Son

Dear Son – I like you, love you, as you are.
But I hold in my heart all the sons you've been
over the years – and like and love them all.

PAMELA DUGDALE

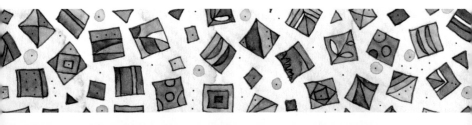

For my special Son

Go on astonishing us!
We wish you
courage and hope
and curiosity.
And love.

PAM BROWN

For my special Son

How I worshipped that boy!
He was like a fantastic fulcrum, around which
our uncertain world could tilt and turn.
It was incredible to me, and quite wonderful,
the way our entire household pulsed to his doings,
the way he could fill a room even in his sleep.
He was everything – my flesh,
my love, my hope for the future.

ANTHONY QUINN

For my special Son

Thank you
for filling a place in my life
that no one else could.

PETER GRAY

For my special Son

I showed you the world through my eyes.
Now you show it to me through yours.

ODILE DORMEUIL

For my special Son

It's difficult to explain that feeling.
It's the greatest love affair, an unconditional love.
A protective instinct
was awakened in me.

DANIEL A. POLING

For my special Son

Sons teach you
how to
laugh again.

PAM BROWN

For my special Son

One can't possibly know what life means,
what the world means, what anything means,
until one has a child and loves it.
And then the whole universe changes and nothing
will ever again seem exactly as it seemed before.

LAFCADIO HEARN

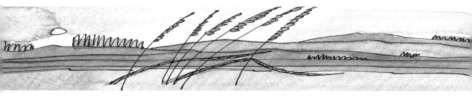

For my special Son

The love between mother and son is like a mix
of steel and elastic. Like steel it is strong
and unbreakable but it will stretch around the World
to wherever life takes them.

LINDA MACFARLANE

For my special Son

I know Josh's friends, his dreams, fears, hopes. What he's thinking, how he's feeling, what mischief he's plotting. What do I live for? The smell of his hair when he hugs me goodbye.
Is that too much to ask out of life?

KATHY LETTE

For my special Son

I have never missed any of the big moments in his life:
his first word, his first step, I was there for them all.
They are far more important than anything
that can happen on the tennis court.

BORIS BECKER

For my special Son

In an uncertain World
I have one constant – you,
my wonderful son.

LINDA GIBSON

For my special Son

I wish you so much.
But most of all I wish
you to be your own self.
To take all the gifts that you were
born with and make of them
marvels of ingenuity
and astonishment.

CHARLOTTE GRAY

For my special Son

Sons go far, take on many guises. But once with the family,
the uniform, the gown, the white coat is set aside.
The great world knows sons by their achievements.
The family knows all his mistakes – all the jokes,
all the adventures, all the habits and tricks and weaknesses
of a lifetime. Dr. Thomas Jenkins is plain Tom at home.

ODILE DORMEUIL

For my special Son

You came into our lives and turned a happy couple into a very happy family. You have grown, our family has grown and our happiness has grown beyond measure.

STUART & LINDA MACFARLANE

For my special Son

We shall build memories, my son
and I, of trips to the seaside, of walks
in the rain, of zoos and carnivals
and theme parks. We shall build beautiful
memories to last a lifetime.

LINDA GIBSON

For my special Son

Every parent cries silently
to their son –
be bold,
be brave –
but be very, very, careful!

PAMELA DUGDALE

For my special Son

Proud parents boast
a little of their son's
abilities and his achievements.
But glory in his kindness,
his gentleness,
his quiet courage.

PAMELA DUGDALE

For my special Son

What's it like having a son?
Well every single day it feels as if I have just
scooped the jackpot on the lottery.

BRIAN CLYDE

For my special Son

To see one's son
confident and laughing
is life's reward.

HELEN THOMSON

For my special Son

How great I feel when I say "Yes – that's my son."

HELEN THOMSON

For my special Son

Seeing your own baby for the first time is an
extraordinary moment. I suppose partly it is a surprise
– and the baby isn't some hypothetical, inanimate object
as it has been before, but really alive, with a perceivable
identity, face, personality all of its own.
I found it a profound moment.

NIGEL FARRELL

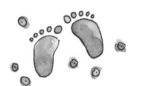

For my special Son

He's got the most amazing smile. You can't beat that feeling when your baby smiles at you. It's just the best.

ROBSON GREEN

For my special Son

Sons have us around
their little fingers
from the moment
we set eyes on them.

AUTHOR UNKNOWN

For my special Son

Take courage.
Whatever you do –
do it well.
We will be behind you.

MAYA V. PATEL

For my special Son

I hope you find
peace and calm
and beauty
all through your life.

HELEN THOMSON

For my special Son

Nobody warned me about the emotion
I would have for Jeremy. When he was a baby,
it wasn't just a cuddly mummy thing,
it was a tidal wave of passion that floored me.

LESLEY GARRETT

For my special Son

He is always pushing himself to the limits,
always striving towards his next goal.
In so many ways he is a true inspiration.

BRIAN CLYDE

For my special Son

With all of the fabulous adventures
I have had, it has been our friendship and trust
that have been the biggest gift.

ALI MACGRAW

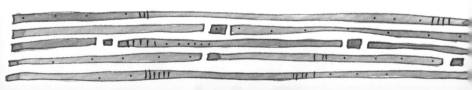

For my special Son

Becoming a dad just feels so right. I've discovered something very different in life. The best investment you can give in life is to others – especially to a child. It's a great feeling just investing your time in this little human being, making sure their every need is met and that they're loved.

ROBSON GREEN

For my special Son

It's such a powerful connection;
it takes me by surprise. I feel like there's a dotted line
connecting me to my son.

SARAH LANGSTON

For my special Son

I HOPE HAPPINESS
SEARCHES YOU OUT
– EVEN ON THE MOST
ORDINARY DAY.

CHARLOTTE GRAY

For my special Son

It's only recently that I've come to recognise
that my son has given my life a sense of purpose,
a focus that it did not really have before.

BORIS BECKER

For my special Son

M y Dear Son...
We had wanted you and waited for you, imagined you
and dreamed about you and now that you are here no dream
can do justice to you... Your coming has turned me upside down
and inside out. So much that seemed essential to me has,
in the past few days, taken on a different colour.

FERGAL KEANE

For my special Son

When nothing's gone right all day and you're feeling the weight of every failure, it only needs the rush of small feet pounding down the path, a leap, arms locked about you, a grin, a pouring out of the day's news – and everything goes your way.

ODILE DORMEUIL

For my special Son

Thank you for putting
exclamation marks in my life.

PAM BROWN

For my special Son

I flicked on my answering machine.
What should I hear but the voice of my son Steve...
I cannot tell you how hearing his voice,
his concern, his good humor, made me feel.
I wanted him right there...

LAUREN BACALL

For my special Son

The closeness was tangible.
The strength of my feeling for him
was staggering. I ached
for the years we had been apart,
for not being there when he
needed someone. But it isn't too
late. He wants me in his life.

CHARLOTTE ROE

For my special Son

May you astonish yourself
in discovering all that you can do!

CHARLOTTE GRAY

For my special Son

We feared that we might not be strong enough to adequately care for our 'special needs' son. But he has taught us, through his patience, love and joy, that together we are one fabulously strong family.

AMANDA BELL

For my special Son

From the day he was born, my life changed.
The happiness I get from him is everything to me now.
I pushed aside all the stupid little things
that I used to complain and worry about.
I realised that none of that matters at all.
Life – the gift of life – is what matters.

WARIS DIRIE

For my special Son

Inevitably a son grows up and leaves the family home.
This should not be seen as a loss or a gap in your life.
Rather it should be viewed as a growth, as an expansion
of the strength and horizons of the family.

STUART & LINDA MACFARLANE

For my special Son

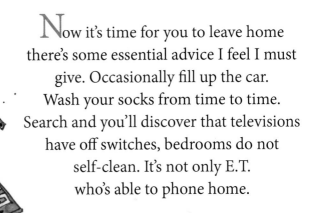

Now it's time for you to leave home
there's some essential advice I feel I must
give. Occasionally fill up the car.
Wash your socks from time to time.
Search and you'll discover that televisions
have off switches, bedrooms do not
self-clean. It's not only E.T.
who's able to phone home.

BRIAN CLYDE

For my special Son

However low I am,
a note or a text
from you brings me
happiness.

PAMELA DUGDALE

For my special Son

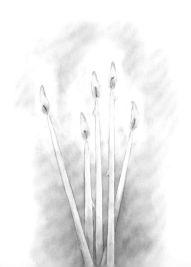

Mankind owes
to children the best
it has to give.

UNITED NATIONS DECLARATION

For my special Son

Dear Son,
May every year ahead be richer in happiness
and personal growth.
And every birthday better than the one before.

ODILE DORMEUIL

For my special Son

Every mother loves her son.
But how many can truly say I trust him,
I like him, I respect him, I admire him?
Only one – me.

LINDA MACFARLANE

For my special Son

Life presents no greater privilege,
no greater pleasure, than the opportunity
to share one's son's childhood.

LINDA GIBSON

For my special Son

Is there anything so wonderful as being the mother of a son? I simply sing, and laugh, and live – oh, how I live the long days through. I have happiness enough for all the world...

KWEI-LI

For my special Son

Son, husband, and now father.
Grown suddenly in strength
and dignity. In love.
In tenderness.
His newborn child so small,
so safe in his folding arms.

KARABO FUNDE

For my special Son

I cradled the tiny you,
I nurtured the growing you.
Now I like to admire
the big you –
my special son.

HELEN THOMSON

For my special Son

Felix is the only person I can row with for days
without things turning nasty.
We keep a running argument up for ages
and then we start laughing.

JILLY COOPER

For my special Son

A son is the guy who flings himself.
He bounces, bumps, ducks, dives, slides,
pounds, paddles, fidgets and falls.
Then he picks himself up
and does it all again.

PAMELA DUGDALE

For my special Son

Thank you for so many things.
For helping me to plant oak trees.
For holding me when I am sad.
For laughing with me when I am stupid.
For believing in me.
For making my life worth living.

HELEN THOMSON

For my special Son

I am proud of you.
Proud of who you are and everything
you have achieved.

LINDA GIBSON

For my special Son

There is a warmth between mother and son,
a kind companionship, a quiet caring.
That does not fade with distance or with age.

JANE SWAN

For my special Son

Parents are very proud if they produce geniuses.
Or astounding, whirlwind celebrities,
who are mobbed and quoted and photographed.
But they're rather relieved if they haven't!

ODILE DORMEUIL

For my special Son

A man should never walk
in the footsteps of his father.
Instead they should walk together,
side by side.

BRIAN CLYDE

For my special Son

He makes me laugh
and I feel through him
that the world
can be a wonderful place.

PETER HOWARTH

For my special Son

If I could give you anything
it would be a quietness
at the very heart
of your life that would
remain tranquil
and certain whatever befell.

PAM BROWN

For my special Son

From the very beginning you were full of
enthusiasm for life. You would wake
at 6 am and the fun and games and adventures
would begin. Decades on and nothing has
changed, you pack a week's worth of excitement
into every single day. I so love you for that –
for being you.

AMANDA BELL

For my special Son

Sons are a good investment.
They mow the lawn
when your back has gone.

CHARLOTTE GRAY

For my special Son

Parents glow a little when people say,
"Isn't he handsome?
Isn't he charming?
Hasn't he done well?"
But they treasure forever
"Isn't he kind?",
"He always remembers...",
"I'd trust him with my life."

PAM BROWN

For my special Son

Sons flash their headlights
when they leave. It means a lot to the
shadow standing at the window.

PETER GRAY

For my special Son

And so, at 5:55 pm a child was born. Our son. So small.
So helpless. We were, of course overjoyed.
But we could never have imagined at that time just what
amazing joy he would bring to the rest of our lives.
We became a family and were complete.

STUART & LINDA MACFARLANE

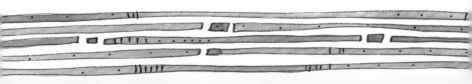

For my special Son

A son is... the voice who reverses
the telephone charges from Morocco and says
he knows you will not mind.
(Which, of course, you don't.)

ODILE DORMEUIL

For my special Son

The world has need of you. Your voice, your touch,
your skills, your understanding.
There has never been anyone exactly like you since the world began.
You are special. You are valuable. Remember.

PETER GRAY

For my special Son

Time passes so quickly, one minute
you were crawling around the house
bumping into things, the next
you have your drivers licence
and driving around town
bumping into things.
Time passes –
nothing else changes.

AMANDA BELL

For my special Son

May the coming years bring you new hopes,
new beginnings, new adventures, new discoveries.

CHARLOTTE GRAY

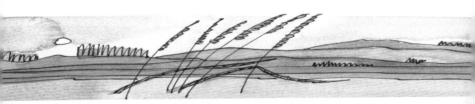

For my special Son

I'd prefer it if they didn't do such a good imitation of Cro-Magnon Man. I'd like them to clean up after themselves more. Yet I understand the male mechanism that drives them out to play. Sometimes I wish I could go with them.

CINDY BLAKE

For my special Son

May you always be necessary to someone.

EDDIE MOLEFE

For my special Son

I wave you away
and stand here watching
till you're out of sight.
Yet part of me goes with you,
sharing all that you experience.
Delighted by your joy.
Amazed by your adventures.
Send me a postcard,
or two or three...

KARABO FUNDE

For my special Son

With your cheery personality and your positive outlook you are a constant inspiration to me. You have opened my eyes, opened my life to a world of adventure and excitement.

BRIAN CLYDE

For my special Son

That's my boy. Ice cream
for breakfast then he
puts on a smart suit
and off he goes to do
his job as a senior lawyer.

LINDA GIBSON

For my special Son

It is gone before you know it.
The fingerprints on the wall appear higher and higher.
Then suddenly they disappear.

DOROTHY EVSLIN

For my special Son

Thank you for your vast
determination.
Your triumphs over gravity.
Your mastering
of skills. Your trust.
Your welcoming.
Your love.

PAM BROWN

For my special Son

WITH EVERY YEAR

THE HAPPINESS YOU GIVE

GROWS GREATER

AND STRONGER.

STUART & LINDA MACFARLANE

For my special Son

Sons bring you gifts from the heart.
Drooping dandelions. Half eaten apples.
Daffodils. Pop-eyed plaster pug dogs.
Strange scent. Hugs.

PAMELA DUGDALE

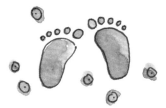

For my special Son

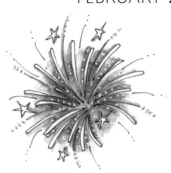

But when my little boy
holds his hands out for me
or is kissing me goodnight,
I feel like I'm in heaven.
Nothing else really matters.
I just feel so much for him.

BORIS BECKER

For my special Son

Boys are a tribe with their own set of rules.
Like football supporters determined to maintain their
image, they swagger and swear and scream at the referees –
except that, in this game, the refs are the parents.
They invade the house like a pack of ravenous wolves,
clear out the food, and, after asking for a tenner, move onto
more entertaining pastures – like the pub or snooker club.

CINDY BLAKE

For my special Son

A son leaves home and there's a gap
in one's life that will never completely close.

HELEN THOMSON

For my special Son

It's quiet in the house very quiet.
The snowstorm wails, the dogs curl up noses
under their tails, my child sleeps, mouth open,
belly rising and falling... It is strange if I cry for joy?

AUTHOR UNKNOWN

For my special Son

Watching you grow
day-by-day,
birthday by birthday,
fills me with pride.

LINDA GIBSON

For my special Son

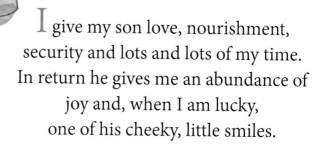

I give my son love, nourishment,
security and lots and lots of my time.
In return he gives me an abundance of
joy and, when I am lucky,
one of his cheeky, little smiles.

LINDA MACFARLANE

For my special Son

Even on the worst days, we usually managed to find
something to smile over, knowing by now what every parent
sooner or later figures out, that these wondrous days
of early parenthood – of diapered bottoms and first teeth
and incomprehensible jabber – are but a brilliant,
brief flash in the vastness of an otherwise ordinary lifetime.

JOHN GROGAN

For my special Son

We are here, when you need to turn to us,
now and always.
Call and we'll come.

HELEN THOMSON

For my special Son

Smiling, laughing, singing...
from his beautiful nature it's easy to forget the big battle
that my superhero son is having to fight.
He is my inspiration and my joy.

AMANDA BELL

For my special Son

I remember, dear Son, when you were eight
and we went on a Great Adventure together.
Watching left and right for lions and crocodiles
and bears and monsters – but we feared nothing.
Fortunately, when we heard those scary noises
during the night, it was just a short dash
across our garden lawn and back to reach
our comfortable beds.

BRIAN CLYDE

For my special Son

How LUCKY I AM

TO HAVE A SON LIKE YOU.

CHARLOTTE GRAY

For my special Son

I hope with all my heart
that you become very, very good at something.
Small or large. Something.

PAMELA DUGDALE

For my special Son

My son. My good companion.
My comforter.
My helper and my friend.

PAM BROWN

For my special Son

A son is...
someone who regards
you as an amiable idiot –
but loves you
all the same.

CHARLOTTE GRAY

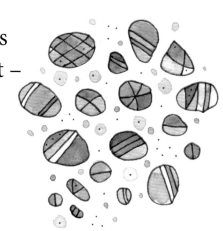

For my special Son

Thanks...
for hauling me to my feet, dusting me down
and getting me going again.

HELEN THOMSON

For my special Son

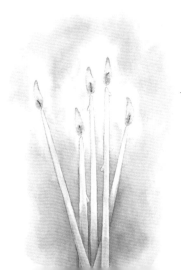

The greatest dreams on earth
I trust to you my child.
You are the seed of humankind,
the hope,
the future of the world.

TRÁN DÜC UYÈN

For my special Son

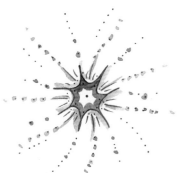

We all need a son…
to give them a cheerful grin
when the world is drab.

PAMELA DUGDALE

For my special Son

I wish you a mind that never ceases
to learn and to wonder, the drive and energy
to work for what you believe in.

PAM BROWN

For my special Son

Our two boys brought us
more joy than we ever
thought anyone or anything
possibly could.
They defined our life now.

JOHN GROGAN

For my special Son

I wish I could ensure you good health, talent, wealth, a good life... And lasting friendships, true love, satisfying work, just recognition, adventures enough to keep your mind and heart alive. But I can't. No parent can. All we do is hope – and always be here for you.

PAM BROWN

For my special Son

Thank you...For taking the effort to choose gifts
that make me smile. For taking the time to ask
"How has your day been...?"
For being there to celebrate my successes and offering
a helpful word when things go wrong.
I could not hope for a better son.

BRIAN CLYDE

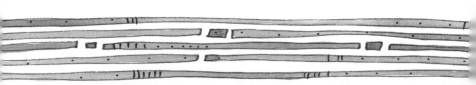

For my special Son

You were my new
beginning.
You have made
my life
worthwhile.

HELEN THOMSON

For my special Son

I'll carry your first cry with me everywhere I go.

PAULA D'ARCY

For my special Son

When my son falls I feel the pain
more than he does. When he smiles
a rainbow glistens in my heart.
And when he finds true love
I feel that my life is complete.

AMANDA BELL

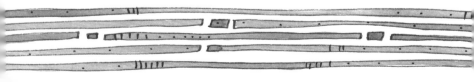

For my special Son

You dream for your son –
imagine his future. Worry about him.
And then, all by himself he maps
his own course and finds
a much better future
that anything you dared dream.

STUART & LINDA MACFARLANE

For my special Son

When you were one minute old,
I thought you were wonderful.
And today, with all the ups and
downs and discoveries and
rejoicings the years have given us,
I still do...
Only more so.

EDDIE MOLEFE

For my special Son

You don't raise heroes, you raise sons.
And if you treat them like sons, they'll turn out
to be heroes, even if it's just in your own eyes.

WALTER SCHIRRA SNR

For my special Son

Memories blur. But, to me,
the happiness of the past years remains alive.
Thank you for them.

PAMELA DUGDALE

For my special Son

Thank you for bringing laughter into my life.

HELEN THOMSON

For my special Son

The door bursts open.
"Look what I've found!"
"Come quick or you'll miss...
a whole nest of spiders!!!"
Thank you for putting exclamation
marks in my life.

ODILE DORMEUIL

For my special Son

A mother's proudest boast of any of her sons
is not his wealth or his success –
but that he is a good son, a good friend.
A decent person.

PAM BROWN

For my special Son

You know that,
if you ever hit rock bottom,
we will be here for you.

HELEN EXLEY

For my special Son

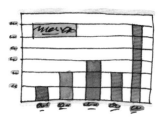

I wish you...

...the ability to turn your skills to mastery.

...the happiness of knowing
you've achieved something worth doing –
small, large or stupendous.

KARABO FUNDE

For my special Son

I WISH YOU WEALTH

ENOUGH TO GIVE YOU FREEDOM —

BUT NOT ENOUGH

TO ENSLAVE YOU.

JANE SWAN

For my special Son

W hen a son has been away, how soon he fits into his old place
on his return. He may not stay – but there is a renewal
in the hearts of all the family. He leaves reassured. There is one
place in the world where he can be accepted for himself.

ODILE DORMEUIL

For my special Son

The other day he fell over and banged himself
and I just felt this pain run right through me.
Ten minutes later he's laughing again,
and I'm wondering if I'm going to have a heart attack,
I'm so worried.

BORIS BECKER

For my special Son

The quickest way for a parent to get a child's attention is to sit down and look comfortable.

LANE OLINGHOUSE

For my special Son

Thinking of my sons,
I see them like a bunch
of beautiful balloons
that I am holding
in my hand at a party.

ANGELA FOX

For my special Son

I am so proud of my boy.
Proud of the man he turned out to be.
Proud of his ideals and values.
Proud and hopeful that, at least in part,
I was an influence on him.

AMANDA BELL

For my special Son

It is best not to venture into your son's toy chest. For there, lurking amongst the marbles, toy aeroplanes and old teddies you will discover wriggly worms and rotting chestnuts and dead mice and fossil poo and broken thingamajigs and...

STUART & LINDA MACFARLANE

For my special Son

A SON IS
THE BIGGEST BONUS
LIFE CAN OFFER.

PAM BROWN

For my special Son

Teaching a son to drive is like teaching
an angry elephant to ballet dance.

BRIAN CLYDE

For my special Son

When you were born the world's
"Joy Index" shot through the roof.
Year by year you developed into a fabulous,
happy, sincere man.

STUART MACFARLANE

For my special Son

Louis is such a joy for both of us and, although it changes
your life so much once you become a parent,
you can't really imagine life without kids. He makes
me laugh and he gives us both so much, he really does.

NICK BERRY

For my special Son

A son is a mystery.
His parents watch him grow with pride,
with puzzlement and with delight.

PETER GRAY

For my special Son

I wonder if you remember how we loved long days
in the country?... How we all put on our bright gloves
and went crunching into the snow? ...
Your tiny boots? I remember. I always will.

HELEN THOMSON

For my special Son

He makes a good life for himself,
far away and you are more than glad – but a little
of your heart goes with him.

CHARLOTTE GRAY

For my special Son

People need a son to scrunch through pebbles at their side
and challenge them to skimming stones along the waves.
To walk through woods and stand and listen for the stirrings
in the silences. To explore the innards of an engine.
To name the stars that prickle a frosty sky.
To know they're there just as long as they're needed.

PETER GRAY

For my special Son

When I am upset I can just walk into a room where he is and he sees me and hugs me and all my woes are like a cliff tumbling into the sea, quite gone.

SALLY EMERSON

For my special Son

...Whoever said it first spoke
with insight and wisdom:
you don't own children,
you only borrow them.

ANNE LINN

For my special Son

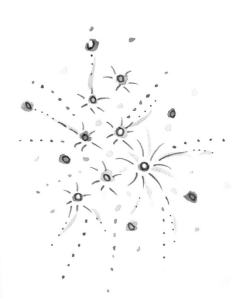

…look upon parenthood
with a sense of mystery and awe.
You are given the joy
of watching life afresh,
and the chance to help
another being take flight
into the richness and mystery
of life. The very clay of which
our world is made is,
for a brief moment, placed
in your hands.

KENT NERBURN

For my special Son

May there always, always be something you want to learn, something you want to do, somewhere you want to go, someone you want to meet. May life never grow stale.

KARABO FUNDE

For my special Son

This world is very small.
However far you go – you will be remembered
and loved.

EDDIE MOLEFE

For my special Son

Everyone should have a son…
– to give them unexpected hugs.
– to lure them into adventures
– to widen their minds
("OK – so it's hip-hop. Just let the music sink into your bones.")
– to teach them patience
("I'll do it later, I swear I will.")
– to love.

PAM BROWN

For my special Son

Seeing your first steps.
The kite we never could fly.
Your first day at school.
Watching you lift your first trophy.
Ironing your first real shirt.
These are my most
precious memories.

LINDA MACFARLANE

For my special Son

You CALLED
TODAY
AND THE SUN
CAME OUT.

CHARLOTTE GRAY

For my special Son

A son is... Toffee. Cogwheels. Pebbles.
Dinosaurs. Bitten pencils. Bikes and beetles.
Hair gel. Boots and T-shirts. Single socks.
After shave. Cars.

PAMELA DUGDALE

For my special Son

Sons never seem to listen and one sighs
and dismisses one's advice as so much wasted breath.
Only to be caught up short one day by a statement
that has an oddly familiar ring.
He is quoting an impeccable source
to back his argument – you!

ODILE DORMEUIL

For my special Son

A mother is proud of a son who works hard, passes
his examinations, does well in his job, is capable and kind.
But proudest of all when she sees him in a happy marriage,
laughing with his little child, sitting by its bed in sickness,
telling it good night tales, teaching it a skill...
loving and beloved.

HELEN THOMSON

For my special Son

Son, this world
is a beautiful place.
Find your perfect place
on it, surround yourself
with loving people,
do all the things that you
love to do. Live your dream.
Be happy.

LINDA GIBSON

For my special Son

All boys like a bit of rough and tumble, to chase ducks, throw stones and maybe even 'accidentally' smash the occasional window. Amazingly they grow up to become politicians and lawyers and bankers... some even become respectable citizens!

LINDA GIBSON

For my special Son

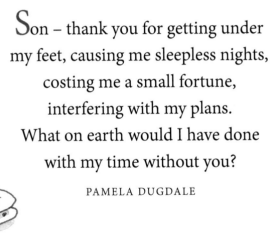

Son – thank you for getting under my feet, causing me sleepless nights, costing me a small fortune, interfering with my plans. What on earth would I have done with my time without you?

PAMELA DUGDALE

For my special Son

The TV drama is reaching its climax.
The telephone rings. Cursing inwardly,
you reach for the phone. It's your son.
So who cares about who did the murder?

ODILE DORMEUIL

For my special Son

...and here you are – kind and loving,
sensible and imaginative. The very best
of sons. The very best of men.

HELEN THOMSON

For my special Son

Like all past parents,
I send you on your way,
confident in all you
are and all you will become.
This is your time.
Delight in all it brings.
Things beyond imagination.

PAM BROWN

For my special Son

Good luck in all you do!

JANE SWAN

For my special Son

To love, nurture, discipline,
and support one's child's growth
requires a perspective
that challenges
the full scope of one's humanity.

ALVIN F. POUSSAINT

For my special Son

When a son comes home for the weekend it is worse than a visit from a swarm of locusts. In his path of destruction no item of food or drink will be left intact.

STUART AND LINDA MACFARLANE

For my special Son

I am blessed to have a son
like you. You are kind,
caring and considerate –
always ready to give
a helping hand.
You fill my life with joy.

AMANDA BELL

For my special Son

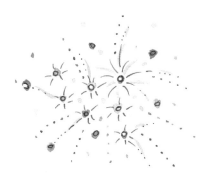

YOU ARE A SOURCE OF SILLY SURPRISES,
UNEXPECTED HUGS, LAUGHTER, COMFORT.

PAMELA DUGDALE

For my special Son

Some day, my son, I hope you know
The joy of watching a small boy grow.
A boy whose laughter makes you warm...
Who gives keen purpose to your life,
Who compensates for each day's strife.
All this I wish so you may know
The joy I had in watching you grow.

EMILY CAREY ALLEMAN, 1893 – 1990

For my special Son

You are on an exciting journey of discovery.
Your whole life stretches before you.
Make the most of each year, each day, each moment.
And, whatever you choose to do, do it well. Do not be
afraid to pursue whatever brings you happiness.

BRIAN CLYDE

For my special Son

Nothing is more important. It doesn't matter
what my day is like or what I have to face,
my son is first and I want him to see me as strong
and positive. It's not always how I feel
but I make myself into that for him.

HEATHER SMALL

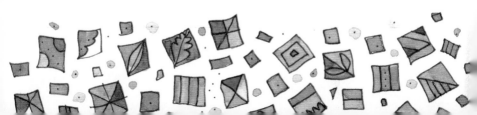

For my special Son

Thank you for demanding
to carry my backpack,
when you were only seven years old.
Because you somehow knew
I had MS – long before even
the doctors knew.
And thank you for your love and
strength ever since.

HELEN THOMSON

For my special Son

You have gone from howling baby to handsome young lad in what seems like the blink of an eye. How you have grown and matured. How special you have become.

MATHILDE FORESTIER

For my special Son

A son can be guaranteed
to astound you all through
his life – astound,
bewilder,
unnerve,
flabbergast...
You name it. He'll do it.

CHARLOTTE GRAY

For my special Son

Wife, the Athenians rule the Greeks,
and I rule the Athenians, and thou me, and our son thee;
let him then use sparingly the authority which makes him,
foolish as he is, the most powerful person in Greece.

THEMISTOCLES. C.523 B.C. – C.458 B.C

For my special Son

I picked him up and held him to me, naked and dripping, but he kept his face buried in my neck. I whispered in his ear, my heart swelling as he gripped me tightly with both arms and legs, still not making a sound. Nothing that happened to me all year was more important than that.

CHARLTON HESTON

For my special Son

A dull day grows instantly bright
when you send me a text.

CHARLOTTE GRAY

For my special Son

I share your joys
and successes –
but never forget
I'm here for you when
things go wrong.

PAM BROWN

For my special Son

What do I wish you? Strength.
Not necessarily of body – but of mind and heart.
Strength to endure when hope has dwindled,
when those you thought believed in you have turned away,
when love has failed.

PAM BROWN

For my special Son

"My son!"
What simple, beautiful words!
"My boy!"
What a wonderful phrase.

CYRIL MORTON THORNE

For my special Son

My son constantly asks questions. What is this?
Where is that? How do those work? Sometimes
I feel as if I am a walking – talking combination of Google,
Wikipedia and Just-Make-It-Up.

BRIAN CLYDE

For my special Son

My son disappears to South America and I get nothing but a postcard for six months, and yet when there's a telephone message that he's arriving at 3pm on Wednesday, he knows – and I know – that I'll be there to meet him at the airport.

PENNY VINCENZI

For my special Son

A child enters your home and makes
so much noise for twenty years
you can hardly stand it –
then departs, leaving the house
so silent you think you will go mad.

DR. JOHN ANDREW HOLMES

For my special Son

The real true meaning of life is your family,
the love that you have, the respect,
the traditional ways, carrying on with them.
You don't have to be rich to have these things;
you can't buy them.

ETHEL WILSON

For my special Son

We look at the World through different eyes, you and I.
You see horizons that are further off than mine –
more exotic, more exciting. It delights me that your life
will be so much more interesting than mine.
It pleases me that I will walk with you for some
of your journey, at least until we reach my horizon.

STUART MACFARLANE

For my special Son

A Cyclist is a man whose son
is home from college.

AUTHOR UNKNOWN

For my special Son

I really wasn't prepared
for how I feel.
I catch myself
looking at him and my eyes
well up with tears.

LYNDA LA PLANTE

For my special Son

I have a little addition on my list of
hopes for you. It's something
for me. However wise and successful
and happy you become – send me an
e-mail, a letter now and then.

ODILE DORMEUIL

For my special Son

My son...You have my blue grey eyes, you share
my wonder and exhilaration in wind and mountains...
You are bone of my bone, flesh of my flesh,
you have my heart as I have yours.

HELEN THOMSON

For my special Son

Sons lose their brand-new sports kits, sons scratch the car.
Sons are grubby, noisy, moody and untidy – and always late.
They keep this up till their parents are plotting deportation
over their evening cocoa – and then, suddenly,
sons give themselves a shake, everything falls neatly
into place – and they stand revealed as reasonable and
personable young men.

EDDIE MOLEFE

For my special Son

I do not know where you will go,
what you will do,
whom you will love.
But I stand ready to applaud.

PAMELA DUGDALE

For my special Son

YOU HAVE MY LOVE

AND PRIDE AND CARE.

ALWAYS.

HELEN EXLEY

For my special Son

From the moment you were born I have done
my best to wrap you in the warm protection of love.
Now that I am growing older, I feel the love
and joy of your protection wrapped around me
like a forever hug.

LINDA GIBSON

For my special Son

There is a special smile that mothers
have when their tall, grown offspring
are home. Even for a few hours.
Utter contentment.

PAMELA DUGDALE

For my special Son

Wherever you are -
in city street or in the hush
and glimmer of a summer wood
- our love is with you.
It shines in the quiet pool.
It wheels above you
in the flight of geese.

ODILE DORMEUIL

For my special Son

Thank you for the train rides

and the roller-coasters.

Thank you for running

with me in the rain.

And sprawling with me

in the summer sun.

CHARLOTTE GRAY

For my special Son

...when you come home
at night with only shattered pieces
of your dreams,
your little one can mend them
like new with two magic words –
"Hi Dad!"

ALAN BECK

For my special Son

Explore the bits of the world
I never got to,
read the books I never read.

PAM BROWN

For my special Son

Sons – they beat you in every game,
tease you constantly, ignore everything
you say and yet, irrationally,
you love them completely.

AMANDA BELL

For my special Son

The only acknowledgment you'll receive
that your son actually did listen
to your advice is when, forty years later,
you overhear him giving the exact same
advice to his son!

BRIAN CLYDE

For my special Son

A son is...
– the one who regards you as the totally reliable
source of shirts.
– the amiable one who wants to do everything for you.
It's just getting round to it.
– the fellow with all the friends
that you find sleeping on the living room floor.
– the boy who says things that drive
his parents to the edge – but smiles at exactly
the right moment.

PAM BROWN

For my special Son

Once you sheltered
under my branches –
but now you give your kindness
and your strength to me.

JANE SWAN

For my special Son

It's easy to tell
when your student son
has paid a visit home –
the fridge is empty
and the laundry basket full.

LINDA MACFARLANE

For my special Son

I must not dream dreams
for you. All I can do
is help you make your dreams
come true.

CHARLOTTE GRAY

For my special Son

"My son" – the happiest introduction.

PETER GRAY

For my special Son

The boy was the very staff of my age, my very prop.

WILLIAM SHAKESPEARE, 1564 - 1616

For my special Son

I celebrate all you are,
all you've accomplished, all the
happiness you've given to me.
May the coming years bring you
more sun than showers.
More joy than disappointments.
Surprises. Excitements. Friendship.
Love.

CHARLOTTE GRAY

For my special Son

Near or far from me
you give me hope and
happiness.

PETER GRAY

For my special Son

To see your smile is happiness for me.

EDDIE MOLEFE

For my special Son

It is best not to let the mind linger
on the state of one's son's bedroom.

MAYA V. PATEL

For my special Son

There can be nothing more joyful
on this Earth,
no activity more precious,
than running around aimlessly
in a park playing football
with your darling son.

BRIAN CLYDE

For my special Son

You can get him out of your study,
but you can't get him out of your mind.
Might as well give up – he is your captor,
your jailer, your boss and your master –
a freckled-faced, pint-sized,
Cat-chasing bundle of noise.

ALAN BECK

For my special Son

...And now you're gone.
Settled happily.
Learning extraordinary things.
And we are so proud of you
and glad you're happy.
But this house has
an emptiness about it.
I miss your clutter.
I miss your chatter.
I miss you.

JANE SWAN

For my special Son

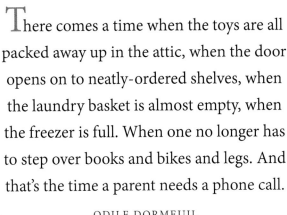

There comes a time when the toys are all packed away up in the attic, when the door opens on to neatly-ordered shelves, when the laundry basket is almost empty, when the freezer is full. When one no longer has to step over books and bikes and legs. And that's the time a parent needs a phone call.

ODILE DORMEUIL

For my special Son

There are three giant boxes of photographs
taken over your childhood. They are
wonderful mementoes but mere snapshots.
Frozen images. Nothing could capture the joy
that you have brought me over the years.
But please know, every moment of it all is
stored safely in the million boxes of my heart.

LINDA MACFARLANE

For my special Son

We made our way together to a big tree on the lawn.
He paused there. Then he took my hand he was
holding and pressed it to his cheek and held it there.
I thought at that instant I would never feel unloved again.

ART KLEIN

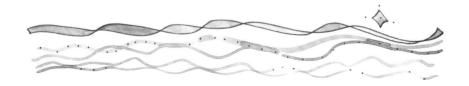

For my special Son

Of course I remember when you were very small.
Of course I have stored up all the things you did and said,
and will treasure them forever. But it is you as you
are that I love. And will, however far you go,
whatever brings you down, or however much you change.
For all my life.

PAMELA DUGDALE

For my special Son

I wish you joy – In love. In life.

PAM BROWN

For my special Son

Thank you for believing in me.
Thank you for being there,
constant in encouragement, wise in your advice.
Giving me the courage to go on.
Whatever good comes of my decisions,
you are a part of it.
Thank you.

HELEN THOMSON

For my special Son

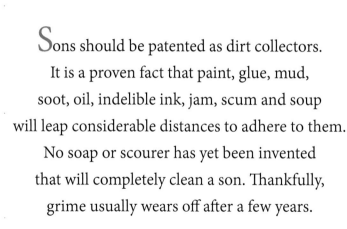

Sons should be patented as dirt collectors.
It is a proven fact that paint, glue, mud,
soot, oil, indelible ink, jam, scum and soup
will leap considerable distances to adhere to them.
No soap or scourer has yet been invented
that will completely clean a son. Thankfully,
grime usually wears off after a few years.

PAMELA DUGDALE

For my special Son

…You spend close
on a couple of decades
preparing your child
to leave you;
you succeed;
the reward is pain.

ANNE LINN

For my special Son

THANK YOU FOR LIGHTING
UP MY LIFE.
YOU ARE MY HAPPINESS.

HELEN THOMSON

For my special Son

However hard the day has been,
the smiling face of a son
pressed against a window pane
is a sure-fire remedy.

ODILE DORMEUIL

For my special Son

What other couples were missing out on was things like; "Daddy, a monster's eaten my holiday", and "Whobody else is coming to my party?", and "How will we see with the dark on?", and "Flowers don't have bosoms, do they" and (a description of water) "Zero colour", and "I'll be nearly four for a very long time"

NIGEL PLANER

For my special Son

He's my best friend,
the one I love most
and know
best in the world.

JANE LAPOTAIRE

For my special Son

One moment in romper suits the next in jeans.
From crawling to driving in an instant,
time disappeared so quickly.
Yet I am blessed to have shared it with you.

LINDA MACFARLANE

For my special Son

I cannot readily explain the romance
of that first encounter with my sweet son...
He was simply the loveliest creature I had ever seen.
Tall now, broad-shouldered, tousle-haired, keen-eyed
and smiling, he remains so today.
I see him and my heart turns over.

ELISABETH LUARD

For my special Son

…there is one place where perfection of the heart is given to us in all its fullness – parenthood. When you look upon a child you have been given, there are no limitations and reservations. You are looking with a perfect love.

KENT NERBURN

For my special Son

I love my stepson as much as I would
had I given birth to him myself.
I am so very proud of him and I feel
so privileged that he chooses
to let me be his mother.

AMANDA BELL

For my special Son

A happy, smiling son is a father's greatest treasure.

BRIAN CLYDE

For my special Son

The first time my son kissed me
and told me he loved me,
it beat all my previous romantic trysts
into a cocked hat.

URSULA HIRSCHKORN

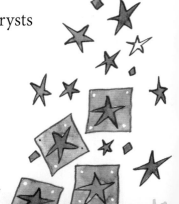

For my special Son

It is your journey.

Good luck.

Ride bravely.

Ride well.

CHARLOTTE GRAY

For my special Son

I wish you joy
in the great things of life
– but also in the little things.
A flower, a bird,
the friendship of a cat.

PAM BROWN

For my special Son

Your first butterfly. Your first rainbow.
Your first dinosaur.
In sharing your childhood I relived my own.

ODILE DORMEUIL

For my special Son

Thank you for making me laugh –
even when I thought there wasn't a laugh
left in the world.

HANNAH C. KLEIN

For my special Son

I love his laugh… it bubbles out in an
infectious wholehearted way.
This is pure joy – nothing else matters.

ANNE MORROW LINDBERGH

For my special Son

Take my love with you
now and into the time
that I will never know.
It is as much a part of you
as breath.
Or your identity.

CHARLOTTE GRAY

For my special Son

Thank you for all your gifts –
all your kindnesses. Like the dead frog
and the wilting dandelions and the mud
puddings. Like the tie-dye scarf
and the clay elephant. Like the pond
you dug, lined, filled and planted
when I'd been lured to see friends
for the day. All of them treasured still.

PAM BROWN

For my special Son

He's a wonderful distraction,
a necessary distraction, somebody who brings
perspective to our lives.

MARION JONES

For my special Son

In that instant he let me into his heart,
and for that I forgave him and the mud
pie he'd built on top of my new canvas
last week, the dump truck loaded
with cow flops I had found hidden in
his closet the day before yesterday,
and all the Spaghettios in his hair
and mine after yesterday's
tantrum-filled lunch.

LINDA GRAY SEXTON

For my special Son

Locked away amongst
our really important documents
you'll find the most
important of all –
your very first drawing.

BRIAN CLYDE

For my special Son

Fatherhood
is unbelievable.
I suppose it's like
a huge wave of love
but much stronger
than that.

GUY RITCHIE

For my special Son

His temper is quick, his tolerance level
dangerously low but when he looks at me
his face lights up. I am the proudest mum,
a lioness with her cub,
ready to fight for him at a moment's notice.

CHARLOTTE ROE

For my special Son

I don't care how many babies are born
a minute in the world. This boy was mine and the only one
that mattered. A divine miracle. He was without
any doubt the most beautiful thing I had ever seen.
My baby, Paris. I was in love and none of the rest mattered.

SOPHIE PARKIN

For my special Son

Visiting, he enters like a tornado.

When he leaves all that remains

is a black hole!

STUART MACFARLANE

For my special Son

My son is a lawyer and I am proud
of all his achievements.
But had he chosen to be an architect
or a baker or a ballet dancer
I would be every bit as proud.
My pride is for him not merely
for the work that he does.

BRIAN CLYDE

For my special Son

The best thing you have given me is your friendship.

PAM BROWN

For my special Son

I realise that my sons
being there, living their
separate crowded adult lives,
yet still and always
embedded in me, is what gives
meaning to my existence.

VICTORIA GLENDINNING

For my special Son

Sons bring you
gifts of love.

HELEN THOMSON

For my special Son

Sons never cease to amaze.
Each year brings new astonishments
and new delights.

ODILE DORMEUIL

For my special Son

I wish I could save you from anxiety and sorrow.
But then – how monotonous your life would be!
So I wish for you courage and clear thinking,
hope and a happy heart. This year – and Always.

PAMELA DUGDALE

For my special Son

Having a baby was rejuvenating
and wild and wonderful.
Being a father is more than I'd imagined.
You have the sense of being on
the brink of being out of control,
and of utter euphoria.
It's what makes life most worth living –
no question.

COLIN FIRTH

For my special Son

One moment you were crawling on hands and
knees, the next you're so grown up.
Time disappears so quickly – yet I am
blessed to have shared it with you.

LINDA GIBSON

For my special Son

Thank you for holding me in mind.

For discovering little things I've wanted.

For remembering my birthday.

For surprises.

For giving an extra sparkle to my life.

HELEN THOMSON

For my special Son

Thank you for scooping me into
every joy and success you've known
and making me feel a part of it.

ODILE DORMEUIL

For my special Son

Do all the things I never
was able to. See the places
I never saw.
Discover things beyond
my understanding.

PAMELA DUGDALE

For my special Son

In spite of the accumulation of signals flagging
the onset of adulthood, nothing really prepares you
for the wrenching moment when your child,
who towers over you and has a black belt in karate,
is no longer yours...

ANNE LINN

For my special Son

I look at my son and I do not see
a shadow of myself.
I see an awesome unique individual.
And I will be there with him
at every step.
Very proud and very happy.

STUART MACFARLANE

For my special Son

He was not born 'perfect' that was clear
from the start. He is 'different' from most other kids.
But he is my son, my glorious son,
and I will love him and protect him and delight in
all the wonderful joy that he brings me.

AMANDA BELL

For my special Son

There is a love that is as pure and precious
as a droplet of water from a mountain stream –
the love between mother and son.

AMANDA BELL

For my special Son

I wish you the gift of love.
Love that survives all trials
and strengthens
through the years.

PAM BROWN

For my special Son

Going to the football together.
Running marathons together.
You are not just my son
you are my dearest friend.

BRIAN CLYDE

For my special Son

You are better than the best!
- The winning goal.
- A shooting star.
- An oasis in the desert.
- More precious than gold.
- More sparkly than diamonds.

You are an extra special boy. Have a wonderful life!

STUART MACFARLANE

For my special Son

Memories have linked our lives
so often and so long
that we are almost one.
I am myself –
and you are totally unique.
Yet we are linked forever.
By experience. By love.

PAM BROWN

For my special Son

Thank you for showing us the world through undimmed
eyes – as bright and exquisite as we had known it.

PETER GRAY

For my special Son

Thank you for laughter.
Thank you for undermining
meaningless solemnity.

PETER GRAY

For my special Son

A loving son carries
your shopping – however silly
he looks, carrying a mop,
a teddy bear,
and a giant watermelon.

CHARLOTTE GRAY

For my special Son

PARENTS HAVE DREAMS

FOR THEIR SONS —

BUT THE SONS

HAVE DREAMS OF THEIR OWN.

MAY THEY ALL COME TRUE!

CHARLOTTE GRAY

For my special Son

Build me a son, O Lord, who will be strong enough
to know when he is weak, and brave enough
to face himself when he is afraid; one who will be proud
and unbending in honest defeat,
and humble and gentle in victory.

GENERAL DOUGLAS MACARTHUR

For my special Son

His friends called round one by one.
"This is my mum," he said to each and every one,
presenting me with pride.
"My mum!" I was walking on air.

CHARLOTTE ROE

For my special Son

Hugh was born on 7 September 1994,
and life, which had seemed like a heap of raw wool
before – a tumble of brier, filth and chaos -
was suddenly spun gold.

NORA SETON

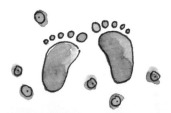

For my special Son

I know some of your dreams.
To drowse on a beach of pure white sand
under whispering palm trees.
To ski in Canada. To shop in Hong Kong.
To sail in a racing catamaran. To ride the moors.
To travel to Venice on the Orient Express.
May you do them all.

EDDIE MOLEFE

For my special Son

We are proud of all
you have become.
We know your strengths
But – never forget!
In case of dire emergency
We're here!

RICHARD & JANE SWAN

For my special Son

I am blessed to have a son like you.
You are kind, caring and considerate –
always ready to give a helping hand.
You fill my life with joy.

AMANDA BELL

For my special Son

From Babygros to suits in a flash.
You have grown and matured before me.
If it were not for the birthdays to mark
the passing years I would not
believe that so much time could
possibly have passed.

LINDA MACFARLANE

For my special Son

If you were awake, I told Isaac silently, you would be
asking me one of your wonderful why questions.
Why are you crying, Dad? After I explained you would say,
yes but why does being happy make a person cry?
My words wouldn't tell you much, but you would look
at my face and I think you would understand.

ART KLEIN

For my special Son

May you find the work, the friends,
the opportunities
and the love you long for.
Meet the future with hope and
courage, enthusiasm, energy and joy.
Take them all and from them
build a life that's worth the living.

PAMELA DUGDALE

For my special Son

You mean more to us every day, every year.
Thank you for being a kind and strong son for us.

HELEN THOMSON

For my special Son

My world would be a drearier place without you.
I am so very glad that you came along!

HELEN THOMSON

For my special Son

I will never forget the first time
I saw you, moments after your birth.
You were wet, sticky and wrinkly.
Quite a few birthdays have come
and gone since then and you
have grown into a handsome,
bright, gem of a boy.
With each year you become
more perfect.

LINDA GIBSON

For my special Son

A son always remembers where you keep Blue Cat!

HELEN THOMSON

For my special Son

All I can do is love you
and be here
for you whenever
you may need me.
Always.

PAM BROWN

For my special Son

May you know the joy of freedom –
and the joy of having roots.

ODILE DORMEUIL

For my special Son

You can do things I cannot do
and I can do things you can't.
And so we make a pair.
Thank you for teaching me.
Thank you for opening my eyes.
I hope against hope
that I can do the self same thing for you.

HELEN THOMSON

For my special Son

Here's your writing
on an envelope and the day
is no longer dull.

PAM BROWN

For my special Son

Sons occupy far more space
than their size would indicate.
That's why the house feels
so empty when they are gone.

PAMELA DUGDALE

For my special Son

I have a total of twenty-two years of absolute joy in having raised my children. I also have their hurt, their pain, and their struggle and that's what comes from sharing in the growth of the family.

DR. SAUNDRA MAAS-ROBINSON

For my special Son

Small boys should come with an on-off button.

STUART & LINDA MACFARLANE

For my special Son

To see you smile
is the best gift I could ask for.

AMANDA BELL

For my special Son

You're leaving me.
Then go in peace.
And let
Your wish alone be lamp
to light your path,
And find tranquillity
where'er you be.

CHAIM NACHMAN BIALIK

For my special Son

Until you have a son of your own, you will never know
what that means. You will never know the joy beyond joy,
the love beyond feeling that resonates in the heart of a father
as he looks upon his son. You will never know the sense of
honor that makes a man want to be more than he is and to pass
something good and hopeful into the hands of his son.

KENT NERBURN

For my special Son

There is one word that is rarely mentioned
between father and son and that is "Love".
But it is there in all the other words that are spoken.
Words about football and golf and music and travel.
All these words are saying the same thing, "I Love You".

BRIAN CLYDE

For my special Son

I smiled joy and he smiled back.
Our eyes held steady, his as clear
and translucent as the marbles
you shoot as a child. Cobalt blue.
Eyes he had inherited from me.

LINDA GRAY SEXTON

For my special Son

The power a child has over you lasts a lifetime.

BETTE DAVIS

For my special Son

You take my love with you
to places that I will never see,
to times that I will never know.

PAM BROWN

For my special Son

WHEN YOUR DAYS

OF ADVENTURING ARE DONE —

YOUR SONS

WILL DO IT FOR YOU.

CHARLOTTE GRAY

For my special Son

He was, truly, a delightful child. Most proud fathers could toss off the same line without thinking about it, but I have thought about it. Often. For years, it was all I thought about. I think about it still, and I do not say it lightly. Christopher was a sunny slice of magic, gifted to us when we needed him the most.

ANTHONY QUINN

For my special Son

I blame Rousseau, myself. "Man is born free", indeed. Man is not born free, he is born attached to his mother by a cord and is not capable of looking after himself for at least seven years (seventy in some cases).

KATHARINE WHITEHORN

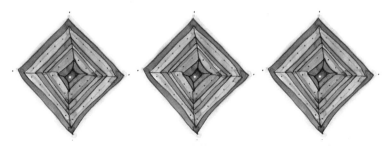

For my special Son

One minute he's your little boy and the next he's giving you a hand replastering – or testing a car engine. One minute you thought he was growing away from you. The next he's your companion.

CHARLOTTE GRAY

For my special Son

Even if a son is in and out
of the house in ten minutes flat,
he leaves behind him
a great swirl of fresh air.

PAM BROWN

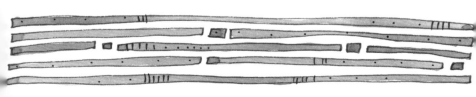

For my special Son

From the very instant that I saw your little feet poking out
from the basket in my room in the hospital on January 16, 1971,
I have valued and respected and loved you unconditionally.
With all of the fabulous adventures I have had in this first half
of my life, it has been our friendship and trust that have been
the biggest gift.

ALI MACGRAW

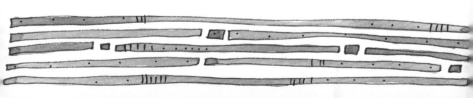

For my special Son

Kids bring a change.
They redirect you.
They teach you
patience and tolerance
and a new sense
of purpose.

MICHELLE PFEIFFER

For my special Son

It may be your special day,
but seeing you happy makes it
so wonderful for me as well.

BRIAN CLYDE

For my special Son

But they do inhabit another country, the young, and
when they speak our language, they do so out of kindness,
translating, censoring when we would not understand...
So I will be careful not to attribute happiness to him.
But this I know: wherever he goes he brings it with him.

SUSAN RICHARDS

For my special Son

There is something very reassuring
in a tall son walking beside you.

CHARLOTTE GRAY

For my special Son

My living boy, my hope, my love, my life, my joy.

GUILLAUME DE SALLUSTE DU BARTAS

For my special Son

Sons leave home, get married and have children of their own. But they never forget their roots, their childhood and where they are welcome should they ever need a hug.

STUART & LINDA MACFARLANE

For my special Son

A boy is Truth with dirt
on his face. Beauty with a cut
on its finger.
Wisdom with bubble gum
in its hair and the Hope
of the future with
a frog in its pocket.

ALAN BECK

For my special Son

THANK YOU FOR GIVING ME BACK STARS
AND FALLEN LEAVES,
WINTER BEACHES, SUMMER WOODS.

PAM BROWN

For my special Son

Sons eat odd socks, shoes, best shirts,
underpants, elastic and combs.
There is no other explanation.

ROSANNE AMBROSE – BROWN

For my special Son

May you have the courage
to choose the difficult.
The will to unravel
the complex.
The joy of adventure
and discovery.

PAMELA DUGDALE

For my special Son

May you always find something to delight you. May you discover what you want to do - and do it well.

ODILE DORMEUIL

For my special Son

If I could bear your pain, I would. If money could buy solutions
or my comfort salve the worst hurts, then they would be there for
you. It hurts me not to help, and it hurts me to know
that all my kindnesses would be inhibiting to your growth.
I'll always be there for you. I hope you know, but you are free –
you must grow away.

HELEN THOMSON

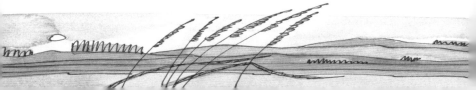

For my special Son

I fell in love with my son
in a way that was entirely new.
You've loved your parents
and then that First Love
and then the man you married...
but nothing like this!

BEL MOONEY

For my special Son

It will make me deeply, quietly proud of you if you can stay
the same and kind and caring in a world where such things
seem less important than projecting the Right Image.
In my eyes you will have succeeded if you're not spoken of
with awe or envy – but with affection and with respect.

PAM BROWN

For my special Son

There are many things I would do for my friends –
but there are limits. With you there are no limits.
I would give my money, my time, the proverbial right arm.
And the wonder is that you never ask, never push.
And the nicest thing is that I know you feel
just that way about me.

HELEN THOMSON

For my special Son

SONS ARE LINKED TO HOME BY INVISIBLE
UNBREAKABLE THREADS — FOREVER.

ODILE DORMEUIL

For my special Son

There is a comfortable kinship
between sons and their parents.
They seem to have a mysterious understanding –
and catch each other's eyes, and grin.

PAMELA DUGDALE

For my special Son

...Sons can't lose.
If we play by the rules, then we're golden;
if we break them, well,
then boys will be boys!

NICHOLAS WEINSTOCK

For my special Son

Sons will never quite forgive you
for giving their beautiful toy plane
to a sad little boy –
even if they're middle-aged!

JANE SWAN

For my special Son

When he clumsily smashes the cups
as he attempts to wash them
I find it amazing to think
that he's a neurosurgeon
and spends his days
performing extremely
delicate operations!

AMANDA BELL

For my special Son

Loved you
the second I saw you.
Love you all the more
with each passing year.

PAM BROWN

For my special Son

I have loved you very much. Loving you was easy.
People warned me about the terrible twos and
the threatening threes and the frightening fours,
but you never had them. You were fun. Wonderful fun.

JOAN BAEZ

For my special Son

He may be amazing.
He may be a genius.
He may be a super star.
But he is just my boy.

BRIAN CLYDE

For my special Son

I loved reading my son bedtime stories –
in fact often I was still reading them to him thirty
minutes after he had fallen asleep.

Stuart Macfarlane

For my special Son

Having a family is like having a bowling alley installed in your brain.

MARTIN MULL

For my special Son

Fly free. Fly high and far.
Your wings are strong.
Great cities are there
for your discovery –
and villages await your coming.
Friends you have not yet met,
Loves you have not yet known,
Marvels and hidden wonders.

PETER GRAY

For my special Son

Sensible sons don't bother
with bouquets.
They send news.

CHARLOTTE GRAY

For my special Son

Like it or not,
we are bound to one another.
It is the lightest of links –
so light that sometimes
we seem to forget it altogether.
But it is stronger
than life itself.

CHARLOTTE GRAY

For my special Son

Wherever you go, we your family
and friends
are here for you – as you are for us.

PETER GRAY

For my special Son

I hope that in your life
you find trust and comfort,
companionship and affection,
love itself. From people
and from the creatures
who share our planet.

EDDIE MOLEFE

For my special Son

There is not one day
of your life
that is worth wasting
being sad.
Be Happy!!

STUART AND LINDA MACFARLANE

For my special Son

We have a lot in common, my son and I.
We both support the same football team and
we both have a passion for long distance running.
But in other ways he is very different from me –
he is his own man. It is these differences
in particular that make me so proud of him.
He is unique and very, very special.

BRIAN CLYDE

For my special Son

Skint knees, bloody nose, fractured bones,
black eyes – just a few of the trophies
my son rejoiced in collecting along the way.

LINDA GIBSON

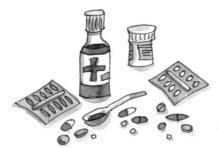

For my special Son

If I could choose to give you only one thing,
I think it would have to be courage.
With it you could face all change,
all loss, all rejection, all failure,
even loneliness. And then build more
strongly than before.

PAM BROWN

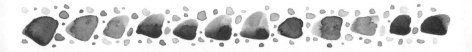

For my special Son

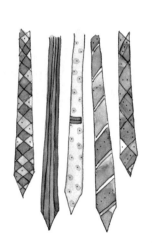

My son is all grown up now and married. But I do not feel that I have lost a son, rather that I have gained a son-in-law. I am so proud of my two boys – the two fabulous men in my life.

AMANDA BELL

For my special Son

My football is really important to me, but my son
and my wife are the most important things to me in the world.
And that's what fatherhood does to you.
You don't realise how much you can love someone until then.
It's a totally different kind of love.

DAVID BECKHAM

For my special Son

The greatest gift I've ever had was the birth of my son.
From the very first, I've always respected him
as a separate person. I've expected to be entertained
by him and I expect to entertain him. But because
when he was small, I knew more than he did,
I expected to be his teacher...
So because of him I educated myself.

MAYA ANGELOU

For my special Son

I wish you love, friendships with both human beings
and so-called lesser creatures, the gift of empathy,
discipline of mind, joy in the mastery of some skill
and boundless curiosity. I also wish you that rare ability
to forgive... yourself, as well as others.

PAMELA DUGDALE

For my special Son

THANK YOU
FOR MAKING
ME FEEL VERY,
VERY NECESSARY.

ODILE DORMEUIL

For my special Son

You've given me a few white hairs,
a good many worry lines,
a degree of exhaustion
– but, too, laughter wrinkles round my eyes
and an unquenchable optimism.

HELEN THOMSON

For my special Son

Long before a mother
ceases to take care
of her son he has
surreptitiously started
to take care of her.

PAM BROWN

For my special Son

The birth of my son brought a little joy into the World.
It became just a little brighter.
A little bit more cheerful. The future will be fabulous
thanks to children such as my amazing son.

LINDA GIBSON

For my special Son

The best thing
in a parent's life
is to see him long after
he has grown and gone,
surrounded by the things
he loves, skilled, useful,
happy – and yet the lad
they've always known.

PAMELA DUGDALE

For my special Son

I wish you the discovery of what you
are really good at and what you
really want to do.
And that you'll have the courage
and the luck that makes
your dreams come true.

ODILE DORMEUIL

For my special Son

A SON CAN BE A TOWER OF STRENGTH
IN TIMES OF TROUBLE.

HELEN THOMSON

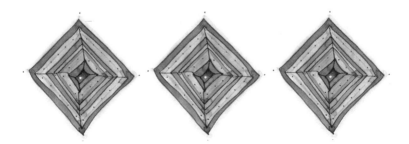

For my special Son

Sons grow so fast.
One minute they are in your arms,
the next on your shoulder –
and, the next, they are striding away.
I love you as you were, as you are,
as you will be. Always.

JANE SWAN

For my special Son

And I remember him putting his arms around me, laughing and comforting me, and my thinking for the first time: This is the beginning of getting old, when my son comforts me. When my son teaches me. When my son looks after me.

VIRGINIA IRONSIDE

For my special Son

This hand of Isaac's, this boy's hand, so primordially and
reflexively fond of hurling stones, brandishing swords, forming
temporary homes for bugs, grabbing, examining, hitting, spilling,
building, curling into different weapon shapes...
This boy's hands could love.
There is a sense of eternal comfort, but you can't express it,
when your heart is in another's hand.

ART KLEIN

For my special Son

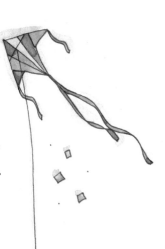

Your birth gave me
the perfect opportunity
to have my second childhood
and I loved every minute of it.

STUART MACFARLANE

For my special Son

My life, at the moment, is a real struggle
with regular trips to the hospital for treatments.
It is my son who gets me through it all –
his smile is much more powerful than
any medication.

AMANDA BELL

For my special Son

My life finished when this little person came into the world.
I started another life. There's no similarity between my life
then and my life now. I feel more grounded now.
There is nothing more important than being a parent.

JEMMA REDGRAVE

For my special Son

Boys commonly gripe about being saddled
with rules and regulations, yet perhaps that's
because they need them. We are boisterous
and brash, fuelled by testosterone...
We stick pencils up our noses, punch
our brothers, punch our sisters, and sprint
around the house when it's time for our baths,
laughing wildly.

NICHOLAS WEINSTOCK

For my special Son

After years of caring for your son,
tending to his every need,
it is a very strange day when he says
for the first time,
"Hold on, let me do that for you,"

BRIAN CLYDE

For my special Son

Thank you for the cups of cold tea
when you were very small
("I found it in the pot").
Thank you for drawings,
and the messages of love.
Thank you for love greater
than I've ever deserved.

PAM BROWN

For my special Son

Knowing you are the most gorgeous, sensitive, loving
and loved boy and you are perfect as you are. Funny, bright,
charming, great dresser, clever serious thinker.
Don't think others are out to get you or attack you –
they're not – just be you.
Yes, you're slightly different and outspoken.
If you have your own mind, it is a huge gift.
Don't lose it ever...

CARON KEATING

For my special Son

When we look at actual children, no matter how they are raised, we notice immediately that little girls are in fact smaller versions of real human beings, whereas little boys are Pod People from the Planet Destruction.

DAVE BARRY

For my special Son

A son who does the housework
is either making amends for something
you do not yet know about –
or preparing you for
an outrageous request.

CHARLOTTE GRAY